This book belongs to:

Mia,   1/3/17

    May all your wishes +
dreams come true!

Love/ Marjolein Bastin

A Secret Sign for Lindbergh

the

Great Blue Heron

Story and Photography by
Margie K. Carroll

Margie Carroll Press
Holly Springs, Georgia

Special thanks to Esther, Doris, Carol and Linda.

© 2010 Margie K. Carroll
All Rights Reserved
ISBN: 978-0-9844793-2-0
Library of Congress Control Number: 2010902578

Printed in Hong Kong

Margie K. Carroll
email: coalcat@mac.com
678-488-5183

Margie Carroll Press
P.O Box 581
Holly Springs, GA 30142

for John and Joan

Hello Friend!

My name is Lindbergh and this is my Mom and Dad.

They made a nest for me on a small island. Dad brought sticks for Mom to build the nest.

After I hatched, Mom and Dad protected me.

My neighbors, the Egrets, had two chicks.

Some days were exciting!

Some days were peaceful.

Ms. Moorhen fed her chick small seeds and snails. My Mom and Dad fed me fish they caught.

Mom and I enjoyed watching our neighbors.

The Egret parents spent a lot of time preening.

My Dad and Mom spent their time flying to find sticks and food.

"When will I fly, Mom?" I asked one day.

"You will need to learn to concentrate, Lindbergh," Mom replied.

"You must also be stronger and older. Be patient. You will fly one day soon, my dear."

I tried to concentrate.
More than anything, I
wanted to fly.

Dad worked hard bringing sticks for my nest. Neither rain nor fog stopped him.

Sometimes, however,
Dad rested in the warm sun.

Over time, I grew and helped out with the chores.

I helped with family decisions.

I disappointed my folks occasionally and I had to hear about it.

But they also noticed my improvements.

"Nice head feathers, Son," said Dad.

I practiced every day, but I couldn't fly.

Dad showed me how to take off and land.
Mom watched with me and gave me pointers.

I felt so discouraged.

"Mom, when will I fly?" I pleaded.

"When a pink bird flies in front of a full moon, that will be your secret sign, Lindbergh. Then, you will fly."

"Thanks, Mom!"

I searched the night sky for weeks.

The neighbors helped me search.

Finally, I saw The Secret Sign!

I lifted my wings and flew!
So, my friend, my wish came true.
I hope your wishes come true, too!
Your friend,

Lindbergh

Heron Facts

The Great Blue Heron belongs to a large family that includes herons, egrets and bitterns. About 60 species make up this family world-wide.

The Great Blue Heron breeds throughout North and Central America, the Caribbean and the Galapagos Islands.

Their habitat is found along calm freshwater and seacoasts. They usually nest in trees near water, but some colonies can be found away from water.

Quick Facts:

Diet: carnivore
Average lifespan: 15 years
Size: Body, 3.2 to 4.5 ft.; Wingspan, 5.5 to 6.6 ft.
Weight: 4.6 to 7.3 lbs.
Clutch size: 2-6 eggs
Egg description: dull pale blue
Condition at hatching: covered in pale gray down; eyes are open and can hold head up

Eggs are incubated for approximately 28 days. The first chick to hatch may become more experienced in food handling and aggressive with siblings.

The primary food for Great Blue Herons is small fish, though it is also known to feed on a wide range of shrimps, crabs, aquatic insects, rodents, amphibians and reptiles. They feeds in shallow water or at the water's edge during both the night and the day. They walk slowly, stand and stab prey with quick lunges of the bill. Great Blue Herons have special neck vertebrae that allow their necks to curl into an "S" shape. That structure allows a lightning-quick strike at prey.

In flight, Great Blue Herons average about 25 mph.

Resource Vocabulary

- adaptability: the ability to change (or be changed) to fit changed circumstances
- brood: term for offspring
- carnivore: an animal with a diet consisting mainly of meat
- clutch: a set of eggs laid at one time
- croak: The sound of a heron call is a harsh croak.
- egret: any of several, usually white herons, characteristically having long, showy drooping plumes during the breeding season
- habitat: the place where a person or thing is most likely to be found
- heronry: Groups of herons are called a heronry
- moorhens: a bird inhabiting ponds, lakes, etc., having a black plumage, red bill and a red shield above the bill: family *Rallidae* (rails)
- predators: an animal that feeds on its prey. Adult herons have few natural predators, but can be taken by bald eagles, great horned owls and red-tailed hawks.
- preening: to smooth or clean feathers with the beak or bill
- plumage: the covering of feathers on a bird
- regurgitating food: Both heron parents feed the young at the nest by regurgitating food.
- rookery: a place where certain birds gather to breed; a nesting place
- Roseate spoonbill: a tall bird (31 in.) with long legs, a long neck and a long spatulate bill. Adults have a white neck and breast with tufts of pink feathers and are otherwise a deep pink.
- soar: to rise or glide high with little apparent effort; to climb swiftly or powerfully
- solitary feeder: individuals usually forage while standing in water, but will also feed in fields or drop from the air, or a perch, into water
- stalking prey: Herons may walk slowly, snatching prey when it is observed. Other feeding behaviors include foot stirring and probing the water.
- talons: a claw of a bird of prey
- wetlands: A swamp is wetland with more open water surface and deeper water than a marsh. In North America, it is used for wetlands dominated by trees and woody bushes rather than grasses and herbs.

Questions for Young Readers

Did Lindbergh have brothers and sisters?	no
What was Lindbergh's one great wish?	to fly
Who protected and fed Lindbergh?	his mom and dad
Did Lindbergh help with the chores?	yes
How did Lindbergh help with the chores?	He helped place the sticks.
Name two of Lindbergh's neighbors.	the egrets and moorhens
Did Lindbergh ever get scolded?	yes
Did Lindbergh ever get praised?	yes
What was the "Secret Sign?"	when a pink bird flew in front of a full moon
Did Lindbergh fly at night for the first time?	yes

Wildlife photographer, Dr. John Flower, first introduced me to a wide variety of Florida birds. We spent many peaceful hours observing the rookeries and nesting birds along the western coast of southern Florida. From our comfortable folding chairs, we more than once accidently napped through important osprey feedings!

John and his lovely wife, Joan, shared more than photography tips and delicious home-cooked meals with me. Their art shows brought them to Georgia several times a year and they tried to "show me the ropes." But art shows weren't for me.

They personify hospitality and are the definition of caring friends. Thanks for sharing your passions with me.

Margie K. Carroll lives in Canton, Georgia, where she enjoys the company of deer, raccoons, rabbits, numerous song birds and several alert cats at her studio in the woods.